Going Numb

J. Hirtle

PublishAmerica
Baltimore

First printing

ISBN: 1-4241-8317-0
PUBLISHED BY PUBLISHAMERICA, LLLP
www.publishamerica.com
Baltimore

Printed in the United States of America

Acknowledgments

During this journey I have been blessed by many individuals who, when joined together, shape my *support team*. Some of these people are mentioned in the text of this book. Others, although not mentioned, were just as vital to me as any.

All scripture quotations were taken from the Zondervan NIV Study Bible. This study Bible has been a constant companion of mine for a long time. Like the comfort received from friends and family, this Bible has provided me with like console while inspiring intellectual growth in the Word of God.

J. Hirtle

Dedicated to
Cameron Dockery
For planting the Seed of Faith
To
Joshua Bolch
For encouraging the Seed to grow

Contents

Preface

My wife is a drug addict. I began writing this journal as a way to release my frustrations, a record of thoughts and events that would be for my eyes only. In trying to understand Tammy's addiction I began to spend many hours reading and researching prescription drug addictions. Along the way I discovered that many people are addicted to prescribed pain killers. I knew those addicts would have husbands or wives, maybe parents or children that were trying to cope with living and loving the drug addict. I thought that by sharing my experiences, my studies of the scriptures and my walk with God, I might help someone endure their journey with less pain than I have suffered. So my handwritten notes scribbled in a memo book were transferred to a word processor, and after much time evolved into the book you now hold in your hands. I hope as you read, the feelings of being alone in your troubles that come when loving one who is addicted, are somewhat eased.

I will share with you my prayers and my study of God's word, how it has brought me comfort and as it relates to my life now; I hope that you will find your own comfort through His Word.

However, you will find sections of this book with little or no reference to God or scripture. These particular excerpts mirror my mood at the time they were penned. It was easy in anger or frustration to look inward instead of upward for answers. Proverbs 14:12 tells us *"There is way that seems right to a man, but in the end it leads to death."* The paragraphs or even chapters that omit God seemed *right* at the time. I know better now, but left them as recorded. *Death* has many layers, physical, spiritual and even provisional. I momentarily died during those recorded moments that excluded God from my expressions and my world. My first words of advice; it will seem to you at times your prayer is useless, producing no response, that reading of the scripture reveals no answers, and that you have finally reached your limit, that your life would be better without the addict included. But always remember—God does care, He will listen, and that He can.

Journal Excerpts

May 7, 2004 (Journal entry) today is James' birthday, as emblematic, living with an addict has dampened another special occasion. Tammy saw another doctor, I can only believe to get another bottle of Vicodin. Does she think I won't see the doctor bills? I have lost count on how many visits it makes this year. I guess she forgot her promise to me to make 2004 different.

May 24, 2004 (journal entry), I told Tammy that we would move back to San Antonio, I told her that she needs help with her addiction, that if going back home was the only way for her to seek that help then that is what we must do. I asked God to help my family. I don't know when I will tell my boss and the guys at work, they have been so helpful and understanding since learning of Tammy's addiction. I feel like I am letting them down, they are like another family to me.

August 4, 2004 (journal entry), we made it back to Texas okay. God provides in so many ways, I just wonder why He hasn't helped Tammy stop taking these damn drugs. She promised me that moving back here would be the beginning of changes. I discovered she saw a doctor the day before we left Georgia! Then after being here less than forty-eight hours she found another free-willing drug-dispensing doctor. God, please help me, please. I never thought that I would grieve this much, not over this.

August 14, 2004 (journal entry) I was hoping for a peaceful weekend, but I screwed up and confronted Tammy about the doctor's visit and about the money used to fill the prescriptions. I wouldn't have done this if money wasn't so tight. Needless to say it turned into an argument. I lost my temper and told her that our marriage was over. I told her that I hate her. I don't, but I said I did. I know my words hurt her.

I am sorry, but too mad to tell her so.

I stopped grieving during the argument, maybe that's the resolve for my grief. I don't know what to do. I pray a lot, but don't think God's listening.

"But now, Lord, what do I look for? My hope is in you."
Psalm 39:7

September 2004

I struggled as to where to begin this story. Although the past may be somewhat blurred after many years of dealing with my wife's addiction, our future is undeniably unclear. My wife's addiction and abuse of prescribed painkillers is in the past, present, and I fear, in the future.

I was compelled to write my thoughts on paper. I am uncertain as to the end of this tale. I believe that in order to tell a good story, a beginning, middle and end are required. I have always enjoyed reading books, anything from a good mystery or suspense novel, to books on the history of mankind, the Bible and books about the Bible. Everything I have read was structured with beginning, middle and ending. (Granted, if I am writing this and you are reading this, the glorious ending depicted in the Bible has not occurred. But the pages, as bound, do conclude.)

Many times, while enjoying a great novel, the temptation to skip to the end would overcome me. This is one temptation that I have gained control over, until now. At this moment I desire nothing more than to skip to the end and see if the villain or the hero claims victory. As you read this, if you are tempted, please turn to the last page and tell me how it ends.

As I sit here today, Tammy continues to seek ways to "go numb." Going numb is her way of describing the euphoria she achieves with her addiction. If I sit here long enough, I can envision numerous endings to this tale. The fact or fiction of those endings will only be authenticated by the unknown future. I am a realist, because of this harnessing trait; I fear the ending will not be the one where I imagined having my family back.

Over the last few years I have spent many hours researching prescription drugs, addicts and their addictions. I researched addictions to alcohol or illegal street-hard drugs. I desired to be as open-minded in my research as possible, and believed that if I narrowed down the research to abusers of prescribed pain killers that I would either overlook something, or become so narrow-minded that I would not recognize any other addiction as that. Regardless of the research subject conducted, I discovered one repeating truth; *rarely does the addict ever gain control.* Dependency clinics proudly posted recovery percentages in the low twenties. Occasionally I would discover a clinic that boasted of success rates exceeding thirty percent, but these were usually followed by an asterisk. Present were articles and books that told of victories over addiction. These stories told of drug abusers beating the odds, and returning to a normal life, tottering off into the sunset. But even these chronicles reflected an underlying fear of the author or addict (sometimes one in the same) returning to the dark world of addiction. Perhaps gradually moving on and elevating to the next harder drug, experiencing greater highs, starting over a new but recognizable secret life. If I sound discouraged, my communication skills are functioning. My imaginations are disproportionately inspired by the thought of sharing a life with an uncontrolled, debasing addicted wife.

It is not my intention to weary you with another story of an addict. If you desire to read such a tale, trust me the bookstore shelves are overflowing with them. My goal is simply to reveal to the reader (and this writer) of how living with an addict affects our walk with Christ. Please don't stop reading now. In order to accomplish this goal, two things are required, 1) an audience and 2) telling the story of an addict.

The requirements of the audience are simple; be a spectator. No further adjectives needed. I hope that in writing these words it will help me and you in learning to cope with being involved in the life of an addict. And perhaps this narrative will direct you to the Truth. The truth I refer to is a life devoted to Christ our Savior. (I pause here, reading my own words, wondering has my devotion to Jesus Christ helped me in coping with Tammy's need to go numb. As stated above, this will be a learning experience for both the reader and writer.) My desire is to always share the good news of Christ whenever the opportunity presents itself. But again, I am a realist. Salvation is an individual experience. Occasionally seeds of hope and faith are scattered by ones you know, or events you experience, or books you read, but ultimately it is your decision to bow the knee.

I stated earlier the past is blurred; it is hard sometimes to remember exact dates or even events. This is fortunate for both of us, if left unfettered this tale would never end. But the beginning of the Tammy's addiction is not distorted by time or a faulty memory.

"From birth I was cast upon you; from my mother's womb you have been my God. Do not be far from me, for trouble is near and there is no one to help"
Psalm 22:10-11

In the Beginning

I often find myself trying to remember what Tammy was like before Vicodin changed her life. I look at old photographs from that time in our life, and I see a happy, outgoing, determined woman. These admired characteristics have been completely obliterated by her addiction. Today, Tammy is always sad, withdrawn, and with little concern for the future unless it involves the requisition of drugs. Her physical appearance has changed also; she looks malnourished, with sunken eyes and is ashen in color. I try to recall the feelings I had for Tammy so long ago. I try to understand how I feel about her now. I have never stopped loving Tammy, not for a second. Regretfully the way I express my love for her has changed, a lot.

It is difficult for me to look at my wife and not see the addict. When I see the addict, other emotions, some, at that moment, stronger than my love for her, reveal themselves with words that hurt, words that cannot be unsaid. Other times I will glance at Tammy doing something as mundane as making a sandwich for our children or brushing her hair and I am overwhelmed with a love that is so deep it will never perish.

I try to hold onto that rush of a feeling, telling myself to take her in my arms and tell her how much I love her, how much I want her to be better, to be done with this terrible ordeal in her life. But I don't. I am stopped by all the feelings that have invaded my life like a cancer as a result of her addiction. I wonder what might be different today, if just once I had ignored my own anger and hurt, if I had taken her in my arms and told her how I feel. My second words of advice to you, dear reader, don't do what I did. Maybe I should write a new bumper sticker; *have you hugged your addict today?*

We have been married for seventeen years now. We had both come from short and ghastly marriages. Tammy had two beautiful daughters from her first marriage, and I had a son, Michael. Tammy's determination as a single mother is what first attracted me to her. Subsequently it was her love towards my son that amplified that attraction. I do remember clearly the moment I fell in love; Tammy had picked Michael up in her arms and hugged him with a hug that God reserves for mothers. I miss seeing those hugs. Five years into the epoch of our new family, Tammy became ill. We were living in Soldotna, Alaska, a beautiful small community, perfect for raising a family. I often felt comfortably isolated from the rest of the world during our stay in the Last Frontier. That isolation did not beget loneliness, as it is want to do. Instead, I felt that the horrors of the twentieth century were thousands of miles away. The vast distance shielded my young children from the onslaught of life-altering temptations. The majestic beauty of the landscape reminded me constantly of the awesome power of God. (I once challenged an acquaintance, a professed evolutionist, to visit Alaska, stand at one of the many lookout points and dare to deny the existence of God. As far as I know he never accepted my offer.)

God was new to me. I was raised in a Christian family, but had decided as a young man, that life was more important than the contemplation of death. Contemplating death is what I believed most churchgoers spent their time doing. Meditation on the death of a Savior and/or their own seemed to be the center of their worship. As a young man, and through most of my thirties, I chose to concentrate more on living, on the present, and ignoring the future. I trusted that there would always be time for God, later. By the grace and mercy of God, he placed people in my life that swatted away my errant thoughts and sinking ground and replaced it with the foundation that has Christ Jesus as the cornerstone, *"built on the foundation of the apostles and prophets, with Christ Jesus himself as the chief cornerstone"* (Eph 2:20). You can say praise God here. But as I am prone to do, I have wandered away from Tammy's journey.

October 1991

Tammy woke me one night complaining of shortness of breath. She had worked in a medical environment for a number of years and recognized there was a problem, a big problem. She told me to call 911; I did. One of the technicians, after a quick arrival to our home, spoke to someone on the radio; I assume at the hospital, the same hospital my wife was employed by. He stated that there was *no breath sounds on the left side*. I was quickly consumed by fear; I could feel the stirring of panic beginning to settle in. Tammy's appearance did not indicate the same anxiety; her calmness during this event was typical of her demeanor then, many years ago now. With the swiftness of highly trained professionals they whisked my wife away. I was allowed only to follow in my car. Late October in Kenai, Alaska, is both dark and very cold, the flashing lights of the ambulance guided my way down the unlit roads and unsuspectingly to a new chapter in our life.

The ambulance's closed rear doors outlined by lights were all I would see for the next twenty minutes. Those doors had not only locked my wife inside, but they also represented the beginning of a life draped by narcotics and the ending of a happy family. Our family was one that had spoken frequently of future plans. We were a family whose home was filled with the laughter of children and gleaming proud parents.

We weren't the perfect family, but that family, and all of the laughter, all of the plans, has been gone for more than a decade.

None of this occurred to me that night. I knew that she was being transported to a facility that could handle this situation. Doctors, after all, know best. That night was also the first time I realized what the Apostle Paul had meant when he spoke of prayer,

"We do not know what we ought to pray for, but the Spirit himself intercedes for us with groans that words cannot express" (Rom. 8:26).

Tammy had suffered a *spontaneous pneumothorax*; a life-threatening condition, her left lung had collapsed and was causing her heart and mediastinal structure to push to the right side. Tammy was numb. It was different than now; this was needed. A doctor-induced numbness.

A chest tube was inserted as I stood next to my wife's hospital bed. Over the next few hours, the doctors would discuss her course of treatment. The options were explained to me.

I listened intently to every word, but could not understand. The doctor may as well have been speaking in Latin. But doctors, after all, know best. So I nodded appropriately, shook their hands, and thanked them for caring for my wife in the best way possible. They readdressed the available options as I waited for them to tell me what they, the professionals, would be doing. They remained persistent in their quest for a layman's decision. Their unyielding quest still boggles my mind. So with reluctance I told him to proceed, without surgery, it sounded like the greater of two evils, and perform sclero therapy with tetracycline; in layman's terms they would glue her lung in place, avoiding future episodes. The doctor assured me that the procedure would be accomplished with little discomfort to Tammy; she would be heavily sedated. However, they thought the recovery would be painful. They said they would control the pain with appropriate medications. *Control,* the one word they overlooked for the next few months.

There was no control. The gates were opened, and they flooded my wife's body with painkiller after painkiller. The drugs were administered with chaos, not control. At one point I did overhear her doctor express concern over the amount of painkillers administered over a six-hour period; the caring nurse replied that Tammy seemed to be in unyielding pain, and it broke her heart to see a fellow coworker suffer so. Only a bystander, I thought, "Doctors know best?"

In looking back time and time again, I wondered why the doctors choose to excessively drug my wife. Numerous schemes have been concocted by my overactive imagination; perhaps they had underestimated the post-treatment pain they warned of, and felt so bad, that the painkillers were for the benefit of the staff as well as the patient (as evidenced by the nurse's response), or maybe they received monetary kickbacks from the pharmaceutical empires when the prescribing doctor reached defined quotas of the selected narcotic. After years pondering their motivation, I have not designed a conclusion. What I do know is what the care providers began that October, Tammy chose to continue.

With that night would follow dozens of late-night trips to hospital emergency rooms. Hundreds of visits to doctors or dentists would be made in stealth-like manner by Tammy. Immeasurable amounts of prescribed painkillers consumed.

Hours of arguments, even more hours of silence, would become the staple of our household and marriage. My knees would become calloused and sore from the hours of prayer; prayer seeking understanding, prayers crying for Tammy's relief from the stronghold of addiction. Our lives changed that night because of the power of a little pill, swallowed over and over, giving life to the Beast.

"They will return from the land of the enemy. So there is hope in your future declares the Lord."
Jeremiah 31:16-17

The Beast

The book *Don't Sweat the Small Stuff...and it's all small stuff* by Richard Carlson makes for great reading and mediation. It describes great ways to overcome small obstacles that invade our lives daily. Unfortunately being an addict or living with an addict cannot be considered small stuff. The good news is that the Bible teaches us that we also need not sweat the *giant* stuff. Joshua and Caleb did not let the giants that inhabited Canaan, a land promised by God, a land flowing with milk and honey, deter them from following the command of God—*"Now move forward. Possess the land"* (Deut. 1:21). The giant Beast that inhabits the life of an addict can be conquered, but we must first *move forward*, we must first understand the Beast.

In 2001 more than twenty tons of Vicodin was manufactured, dispensed and consumed by the American public. Vicodin is a prescription painkiller, a combination of hydrocodone and acetaminophen. Hydrocodone is an analgesic opiate, closely linked to morphine, and is habit forming.

I can only assume that Vicodin is Tammy's drug of choice. I cannot be sure of other drugs that may have been prescribed to her by the multitude of drug-dispensing professionals she has sought out during her journey. Much of the twenty tons of Vicodin was required to ease the pain of the partakers; that I am sure of. Just as I am certain that many abusers of this opiate began journeys similar to Tammy's, prompted by the lack of hesitation of doctors and dentists to prescribe Vicodin or other opiates. Appropriate patient follow-up by the medical professional rarely follows the freewheeling script writing.

Upon entering the body, opiates travel via the bloodstream, arriving quickly in the brain to stimulate the opiate receptors. Dopamine is released, creating sensations of pleasure and reducing pain. What if the addict is not experiencing pain? What if the addict is consuming Vicodin so frequently and in such quantities that any warning pain associated with thousands of common ailments is squelched, the warning going unnoticed? I am not a doctor, chemist or pharmacist, but I don't have to be to know the answers to these questions cannot be good. The opiates simply provide what the user seeks while unknown changes occur within their fragile bodies.

The painkillers are swallowed, beginning their travel to the brain. Their travels will carry them through the complex highways of the user's body, blazing a trail future pills will follow. Upon arriving at their final destination, the painkillers begin their work of numbing the user's receptors to pain or reality. At first the body is unsure of how to react to this new sensation. The relief that was desired has been provided, but by an outsider, a stranger. Designated cells in charge of memory mark this occasion, relief came faster than normal, and the Stranger provided the relief. The painkiller is tagged for recognition, allowing for effortless future admittance.

Over time the effects and purpose of these first painkillers begin to fade, the physical pain or mental anguish slowly returns. As the previously delivered contentment wanes, the addict readies herself to swallow another pill. The body cries to the brain for relief. "Give us more of the Stranger!" it pleads. Other, more rational parts of the brain explain that the pain is not as bad as before, we can easily handle this without the Stranger's invasion. An internal argument, which will be repeated many times during the life of the addict, begins. As Rationale loses the argument, over and over again, the Stranger slowly gains control. Way back, in a small dark fissure, where sound is absorbed by self-erected walls, Rationale weakly objects to the painkillers, knowing that no one hears, no one cares. The Stranger has won. The Stranger is now the Beast, the Beast known as *Addiction*.

Addictions to opiate-category drugs can be both physical and mental. There is not a consensus as to what causes a person to become addicted to drugs or alcohol. Philosophies include physical and mental dependencies, chemical imbalances and genetic predisposition. A person's behavior doesn't appear to get much credit or blame. In our politically correct world we are afraid to place blame. The blame belongs to the abuser. It is the addict's behavior that prompts her to continue to medicate after the need to do so has passed. It is her behavior when she manipulates and deceives in order to insure another script is written. It is her hands that open the pill bottle, her fingers that place the pill upon her tongue. It is the abuser's behavior that destroys the lives around her by causing so many unjust burdens.

The senior pastor at the church I attend is fond of telling the congregation to bring our *bucket of rocks* to the altar. Place our burdens at the foot of the cross, a lesson taught to us by scripture; *"Do not be anxious about anything, but in everything, by prayer and petition with thanksgiving, present your request to God"* (Phil 4:6). What a magnificent gift! To know that our problems are a concern to the Lord, and that by asking for help our burdens will be lightened or even removed. David wrote in Psalm 34:4-6, *"I sought the LORD, and he answered me; he delivered me from all my fears. Those who look to him are radiant; their faces are never covered with shame. This poor man called, and the LORD heard him; he saved him out of all his trouble."*

Regardless of what constitutes the rocks in our bucket, it is important when placing them at the altar that we leave them there. When I pray to the Lord about a problem, if I ask Him for guidance, if I cry to Him for help, it pleases Him.

But if I then rise from bended knee and take my burden with me, if I continue to vex and lose sleep over the weight of the burden, if I don't even listen to my own prayer, how then can I expect God to respond to my words of anguish? How can I then be disappointed when my prayers go unanswered?

Psalm 55:22 tells us to *"Cast your cares on the Lord and he will sustain you, he will never let the righteous fall."* The writer didn't limit our *cares* by describing them as giant or simple, caused by others or self-inflicted or for you or a loved one. He simply stated *cares*. When we obey His word and place or cares, our burdens *on the Lord*, He keeps His promise. When you look up and see the burden is still there, take a moment to look closer and realize that your shoulders are no longer bearing the weight alone, that Christ Jesus is now your strength. Realize that God is sufficient.

The recovering drug addict experiences this dilemma at a much deeper level. They may become sober, their burden lifted, but in the darkest recesses of their mind, the Beast with its own bucket is constantly hurling stones at the recovering addict. The Beast is trying to gain their attention, reminding them, with each rock thrown, that going numb feels pretty good. Forget about the pain of detoxing, forget the hurt inflicted on your family, and forget how perilous the past journey had been. Rock after rock, each carefully chiseled with crafted, lies is tossed at the addict. She remembers the engaging, euphoric lack of sensation that accompanies going numb. She hears his taunts. Then slowly, but almost predictably, the addict starts to believe the Beast. With just one pill, just one drink, just one more high; a relationship begins again. Take one more trip, it's okay, you stopped before, and you can stop again. But as with all burdens, the more they are nurtured and embraced, the more they are encouraged, the more they will grow. As the burden grows, it changes and the burden becomes the master, the controller, the king of kings and lord of lords. The Beast makes his triumph return. And the addict; well, now this once beautiful person is a broken shell, an unneeded weight, weak and pitiful, forgotten, lost in the numbness.

The Addiction is strong and unyielding, this Beast has no need for the addict, the mind of the addict is expendable, and the addict is gone forever, only recognized by the markings of the Beast.

"Since everything will be destroyed in this way, what kind of people ought you to be?"
2 Peter 3:11

Everywhere I Look

Is the person addicted to prescribed painkillers any different than the street addict who pumps heroin into his veins or sucks on a crack pipe and becomes an outcast of our social system? In Tammy's case her addiction to Vicodin spans more than a decade, during which she was able to function in society. She maintained a career, she helped raise a family, and she attended church, she had friends. The obvious differences between the *functioning addict* and the street addict began to fade after years of abuse. With ongoing use the tolerance of either drug of choice begins to develop and their desire to use more increases. Like the heroin addict, the prescribed painkiller addict will suffer through withdrawal if the supply is halted. To continue the supply, the user will go to any means in obtaining the desired drug. Eventually the abuse will adversely affect the career of the addict, resulting in poor performance or perhaps job loss. The addiction defines the abuser's life, regardless of the drug choice. No, there is not much of difference between the two.

During my study, the stories of the addicted began to sound familiar. The stories had a recognizable ring to them that I had difficulty in placing at first. It's like when you know the name of the artist of a great song, but it just hangs out of your reach, taunting you, until at last (sometimes days later) you finally remember the name. I took a break from the research to investigate this feeling. I wanted to know why I felt as though I knew some of the people whose stories I had read. My hiatus was short. Without much pondering I began to realize how many addicts had touched my life over the years. Everywhere I looked, there were memories of people who suffered the pains of an addiction.

My father was an alcoholic. I have fond memories of my childhood, but the ones that could be classified as such, do not involve my father very often. Alcohol consumed him. He lost his legs, his memories and eventually his life to his beast. I recalled attending ALANON as a child, but remember little from the experience. I do remember my mother's insistence that we attend these classes, it would help us understand our father's problem. I am quite sure, during the decades of the sixties and seventies, understanding one's problems was more important than solving one's problems. Some things do not change with time. The only difference now is that we place the tag of *syndrome or disorder* on anything we do not fully comprehend.

Two of my sisters have confessed to drug addictions. I was not with them when they fought their battles. Although they were my baby sisters, their struggles were fought as adults. As with Tammy, the beginning of their addictions has been contemplated by my gray matter on more than one occasion. I often wonder if my actions may have been a contributing factor or even the catalyst to their dependence.

Janet, the older of the two, was once married to my former business partner. He and I had a falling out about the business (falling out is probably too gentle of a phrase). The timeline, as I remember, places the fallout just prior to their divorce, which was closely followed by the darkest time in Janet's life.

Susie worked for me at the above stated business, a nightclub, and frequently stayed after hours, with my encouragement, and consumed the very product that I traded. As the effects of alcohol lost their allure, other, more powerful highs were sought, found and abused.

In both cases, an event or an accumulation of events preceded the addiction. I cannot overlook my involvement in these events. I hurt deeply when I consider that a change of my behavior may have ultimately changed theirs. I apologize to both of you.

My sisters may have a better understanding of Tammy's addiction than I do. Their advice and words of wisdom are always welcome, even when they are flippantly honest. I have searched deep to look for my contribution to the cause of Tammy's decision to choose to live her life as an addict, but have not found one. However, my behavior in dealing with her addiction has not always been supportive, loving or understanding. My sisters have pointed this out to me. The addict commonly practices blaming others for their ruined life. I will discuss this behavior more as the pages progress.

Janet and Susie have both come to know the grace, mercy and the glory of our Lord and Savior Jesus Christ. Janet has gained control of her addiction with the help of God. Susie still struggles, sometimes winning but more often losing. Her love for Christ is apparent; His love for her is undeniable.

Though her battle is fought on a daily basis, it is God's love that has prevented the final step into darkness from happening. I continue to pray and thank God for the intervention in their lives, just as I continue to pray and wonder when He will work the same in the life of my beloved wife.

Other addicts have entered my life along the way, none as profoundly as my father and my little sisters. I spent four years as a United States Marine. Being stationed in Kaneohe, Hawaii, was indeed a paradise. Although what I witnessed, as a member of the greatest fighting machine known to man, was far from paradise. There was rampant alcoholism. Drinking at the E-Club was as customary as daily exercise. The drinking was often encouraged by the senior officers, as a way to relax and momentarily forget the concerns a young Marine, away from home, may experience. It has been almost thirty years since I enjoyed the prestige of belonging to the Corps. The faces and names have all since long faded, but one event is as clear today as it was in 1978.

The Corps did not totally ignore the alcohol problems. When a Marine got in trouble because of his drinking, rehabilitation would take place. I cannot write of the procedures used to reform the drinker, I was never privy to that information; however, a commonly known practice was the administering of Antabuse. A person under the effects of this drug may act adversely if he were to consume alcohol while the drug was present in his system.

A young Marine, on a shuttle to Waikiki, sat in front of me one Friday evening, excited to be starting weekend liberty. I did not know him, or that he was freshly out of rehab. I did not know what was happening when he suddenly fell on the dirty floor of the bus and began to convulse. I did not know what a fellow Marine (also a fellow rehab attendant) was doing when he placed his comb inside the fallen Marine's mouth to prevent him from swallowing his tongue. I did know, and was correct, that the image branded into my mind would last a lifetime.

I began a list of other addicts that have crossed into my sphere over the years. I was amazed at the length of this list:

Brother-in-law—Alcoholic
Niece—Various drugs
Nephew—Alcoholic
Nephew—Vicodin
Best friend's wife—Vicodin
Boss's son—Cocaine
Fellow employee—Alcoholic
Brother-in-law—Alcoholic
Brother-in-law—Alcoholic/marijuana
Church member—Vicodin
Admired radio host—Prescription drugs
Admired football star—Prescription drugs

I ended the list here when it became too discouraging. With some on the list, I discussed the addict's life with their loved ones, people that are in the same position as I. Others on the list were in the far background of my life with little or no involvement in theirs. All of them weigh heavy on my heart.

Everywhere I looked along the timeline of my life, there stood an addict. Is the problem that widespread? Are so many held by the incarcerating grasp of addiction? How many more share their lives with an addict?

"He moves mountains without their knowing it."
Job 9:5

Living with the Addict

Many events in our lives could be considered life altering; marriage, the arrival of a baby, the loss of a child, just to name a few. For my family, nothing has altered our lives as much as living with an addict. Imagine for a moment all the activities of our family life represented by the spokes on a child's bicycle. Each spoke firmly secured to the inner hub, the family unit. From the hub they extend outwards, crossing each other at a precise intersection, providing strength, at the far end attached to the outer rim. God represents the outer rim, holding in place and appearance all the spokes of our lives. The action of the addict eventually causes one of the spokes to come loose from the hub, falling off center. I stretch, trying to grasp the spoke and reattach it to the hub, my family, but it is just out of reach, I try again, but soon I weary from the struggle and with reluctance and sorrow I surrender.

The firm grasp of God's hand on the outer rim is all that keeps the spoke from falling away completely, lost, never to be seen again.

Many areas of our life are represented by the spokes, all of them susceptible to damage by the addict. The obvious damage includes fiscal responsibilities, a weakened marriage and spiritual struggles. Other areas are not so obvious. My youngest daughter has matured beyond her years as a result of witnessing many arguments about

Tammy's behavior or the end results of the same. Children are inquisitive; they pay closer attention to our words and actions than we as parents may think. I have always believed that we must let a kid be a kid. They will have many years as an adult; there is no reason to rush them to that summit. But regarding Sara I have fallen short by allowing her mind to mature beyond her young age. She is too young to be familiar with words like *addiction* or *recovery*. She is too young to worry about Mom *not acting normal*. And yet her tender age has not secluded her from these things. Not always understanding fully, she offered to give me her ten dollars earmarked for the school book club in order to buy Mommy's medicine, this after hearing an argument about spending more money on drugs. She did not understand the argument wasn't about *spending more money*. She didn't understand that her offer made with all the love in her heart would cause mine to break. What she understood was that her mother was upset, that the purchase of the medicine would make Mommy happy again and that she would be able to help with her very own money. This ten-year-old child should have only been concerned with the books she would be able to purchase at the fair. Another spoke falls away, this one cannot be fixed; she is ten years old just once.

Social gatherings are another area that has become like the dangling spoke. Not knowing if Sober-Tammy or Stoned-Tammy would show up, I eventually chose just not to go; it was easier. Trying to explain away Tammy's slurred words or reclusion is too hard.

Changes in my own behavior have occurred. When I am ill, I rarely seek the advice of doctors. I hesitate before swallowing a pill. Even a headache must become severe before I succumb to medication. I will forever view doctors and medications differently. I can find no attraction in either.

In any marriage, dependency on our spouse integrates the relationship. Today, I cannot depend on Tammy for anything. Not because she may be incapable but because the addict is unreliable. Reducing my dependency doesn't strengthen me; it weakens the marriage. Still another spoke falls away.

Living with an addict changes us. Many changes occur slowly, eroding away like the surface of a rock exposed to a flowing river. Eventually the damage is enough to cause each spoke to become unhinged leaving the family with no connection to God.

"Do not stop crying out to the Lord our God for us, that he may rescue us."
I Samuel 7:8

Summer 2003

I am not sure if there is a defining moment in the life of an addict when their occasional need becomes a life-changing addiction. I don't think they know either; their reluctance to recognize the changes in their habit is tempered by the high they receive. I do know, however, when the moment of definition that Tammy was addicted appeared in my life. Much like the addict, I had rationalized her abuse for many years prior to this moment. I believed, as she did, that she was in control; this was something passing through our lives without consequence. Like the stages of life children experience, I thought she too would grow out of this. The summer of 2003 convinced me otherwise.

I received a call from Tammy's friend or a coworker telling me that Tammy had gone to the emergency room. She was complaining of severe pain. She had self-diagnosed the cause of this pain as originating from the gall bladder. Addicts become very adept at self-diagnosis. They spend many hours in the presence of medical professionals, sponging from them all the key components that assure the dispensing of the craved narcotic. Tammy had been to numerous emergency rooms on many occasions with the pain associated with gallstones or an unhealthy gall bladder. On every occasion she received her medication. She also received directions to return for a follow-up appointment to discuss the options she had to rid herself of this recurring pain. She always left with the prized script that would allow her to satisfy her addiction, but she never returned for the follow-up. After all, she knew if the source of the pain were removed, she would need to fabricate a new ailment in order to get her Fix. She always explained away the neglect to seek further help by claiming to *feel better*.

Anticipating the same story, with the same results, I headed to the emergency room. An emergency room is a terrible place. Probably not for the reasons you would think. Although sadness, despair, septic odors and callousness are all common characteristics associated with the ER, to the frequent waiting family member the room becomes an unlikable character in a bad movie. The rooms all begin to look the same, filled with the same "We care" faces. Rooms where clocks move at a molasses-drenched pace. The "We Care People" make it clear that their concern is for the patient, and you are only along for the ride, in the back seat where your view is obscured by their reluctance to tell you anything tangible.

By time I arrived, Tammy had already received a magic dose of a nameless drug. She had also received the first of three diagnostic tests that would be administered this night. Her appearance had become so familiar to me that there was no shock when I was allowed to see her.

The well-practiced grimace on her face materialized the moment I entered the space, an area formed by sheets hanging on hundreds on metal rings. The ER's real rooms are reserved for those dying, or so badly maimed that spectators would become patients themselves if forced to look upon the injuries. A *We Care* person informed me that another test was being scheduled. "What were the results of the first?" I inquired, not expecting an answer. *We Care* told me the results were negative, not uncommon, sometimes the test wouldn't reveal everything. Based on my wife's complaint, the doctor was quite sure the gall bladder was the pickle. I suppose this was *We Care's* attempt to lighten the mood. I resisted telling her that if the doctor were so certain of his pickle diagnosis, there should be no need to order another test. I also resisted telling her based on my past experiences the next better and more expensive test would also turn out to be negative. But not showing admiration and true obedience to the *We Care* people would definitely be the wrong move. So instead, I thanked her and took my assigned post in the hard plastic chair beside my wife's bed. Hours passed before another member of the *Caring Family* came to wheel Tammy away. "We will have her right back, don't worry," he assured me. I knew she wouldn't be right back; no one knows how long anything takes in the hidden rooms of a hospital. And I couldn't worry; I was too tired. I had seen this episode too many times; it would no longer keep my attention.

As predicted, she didn't come right back, and the results of the second test were the same as the first; negative. The reassurances from the staff came as frequently as the painkiller Tammy was absorbing. A third test, even better than the previous, was ordered by the attending physician. As night became morning I realized I had not yet met the doctor who was acting as my warden. I wondered if he was some young, pimply-faced intern ordering tests on my wife in order to accomplish an educational requirement. Maybe he was bitter, having to work these awful hours, and took his revenge on the patients and their supporting family by prolonging the stay with unneeded analysis.

Or perhaps he was the well-worn doctor who listened to the hospital lawyer's recommendations that all available tests should be administered to avoid malpractice tort. Sitting on my hard plastic chair it was easy to entertain myself by imagining the actors in this play as all being the adversary. When I wasn't imagining, I was praying. As the hours passed, I found myself doing less of the latter. My prayers had started off by asking for relief for Tammy, asking our God and Father to guide the hands of the caregivers. As the night slowly unfolded my prayers became more self-centered. I began to pray that I would not be bitter, that my doubts about the sincerity of Tammy's illness would fade to black. I began to pray that I would soon get some sleep.

Suddenly Tammy was no longer mentioned in my petitions. Does God hear all of our prayers? Is God delighted with of our cries for help? As the night lengthened, I realized the answer to these questions. In prayer, in true "I am hurting, God" prayer, "I love you, Lord" prayer, "come to me, Jesus" prayer, he is pleased. But when my prayers became more of a drive-through window request, God heard, but was not pleased. And like every amplified voice at every cheap drive-through restaurant, I could not understand His reply.

As one day became the next, I finally met the attending doctor. He informed me that Tammy had been scheduled for surgery to remove her gall bladder. This decision was not based on the results of any of the tests thus far performed, but on the *classic symptoms* Tammy was experiencing. The surgeon would be able to work her in this morning, and he would likely meet with us prior to the surgery.

The nurses prepared Tammy to be transported to her room where she would await the surgery.

I had been in the ER for fourteen hours. I was tired. Little conversation with my wife had taken place during these hours. Tammy had been scheduled for this particular surgery before. She had balked the last time, chickened out. She wasn't acting cowardly now. In fact she was acting like anyone would who knew that the cause to their pain had been identified and would in short time be fixed by the skilled hands of a surgeon. I began to feel guilty about my late-night selfish thoughts. How could I have doubted the sincerity of her complaint? When had I become so calloused, so shallow, so uncaring? As it turns out, I hadn't.

When we had settled into her hospital room, Tammy asked that I go to the house and pick up personal items she would need for her stay. She listed a number of things, including clean underwear. I told her I would leave now and be back long before they would take her to surgery. I tenderly kissed her forehead and prepared to depart. As I reached the door she stopped me and said something I found rather strange. She retracted her request for clean underwear.

"Don't worry about it, unless there are some on the top of the dresser."

On the walk to my car, on the drive home, and as I walked up to the front door, I turned her last statement over and over in my mind. Why had she said that? Why was her cancellation of this simple request alarming me so much? I climbed the stairs to our bedroom. As I entered our room the dresser was on the left. I stood in front of the dresser, staring at the drawer that I knew housed her unmentionables. I am not sure how long I stood there before I reached and opened the drawer. At first glance everything appeared normal. I reached into the drawer and removed enough clothing to reveal what I knew deep inside I would find. Lying on the bottom, covered by the silk material, were two prescription bottles. Both container labels indicated the contents as Vicodin. One's quantity was ninety, the other was fifty. The prescribing doctors were different. The dates were different; one was a week old, the other four days old. Both bottles were empty. My wife had consumed 140 pills in just one week.

I sat on the edge of our bed, holding an empty bottle in each hand.

The math was simple, twenty pills a day. When she ran out she had headed to the emergency room to re-stock. She was in the hospital now, receiving the supply, satisfying the Beast. I was numb.

Years of suspicions and denials began to intertwine and revolve into a clear picture, into a defined finale. My wife is a drug addict.

I probably could have sat there for hours, turning this confirmation over in my head. I recalled my own past rejection, and chastised myself for this ignorance. Hours would be needed to understand the implications of two empty pill bottles found hidden in a drawer, but I didn't have hours. Tammy was scheduled for surgery soon. I needed to stop the surgery. I sped back to the hospital.

As I entered my wife's hospital room I could tell her numbness had been elevated. Pre-op drugs were the contributor. Why were these necessary? After all, she would be sedated during the surgery. "To calm her down before we put her to sleep" was the moronic reply of the new *We Care People*. Tammy had shown no anxiety towards surgery in all the time we had been in this hospital, yet she had taken advantage of my short absence to convince her keepers that more drugs would be needed. I told the gullible attendant that I needed to speak with the chaplain.

Little time passed before the chaplain's soft knock on the door was heard. I asked him to speak with me in the hallway; Tammy was resting. I didn't know what to say, or where to begin. I managed to tell him that my wife's problem was not a physical ailment, that she had faked symptoms like an award-winning actor. I told him I believed my wife was an addict. Before I could say more the nurse tapped me on the shoulder and informed me they were taking Tammy to surgery. As I looked back I saw a medical team wheeling Tammy away. The chaplain had said nothing, I looked in his eyes and saw true concern, on his face I read helplessness; he couldn't stop the wheels that were rolling. I followed my wife.

In the small room where they prep the patient for surgery I would discover the power of the spoken word. In this eight-foot by ten-foot room lay my desperate wife, three nurses and I. Nurse number one focused all her attention on Tammy. Nurse number two asked me if I had any questions.

"Yes, I would like to speak with the surgeon."

"Well, he is preparing for your wife's surgery, but I can try to answer your questions."

"No thank you, I need to speak with the surgeon."

"Why?"

"I don't think my wife needs this operation."

Powerful words! Everything in the room stopped. Nurse number one turned her attention from Tammy to me. Nurse number two acted as if I had spat on the Golden Surgeon's Idol. Nurse number three said she would get the surgeon. If someone had walked into the room during the next five minutes they may have believed that all the remaining occupants were as numb as the patient. The heaviness caused by my statement increased with each passing second. I felt as if I would be crushed, flattened into an unrecognizable shard, to be swept up and tossed away by the efficient housekeeper.

The surgeon arrived like the hero in an old cowboy flick. As a matter of fact he resembled a John Wayne character. If there had been swinging saloon doors to the room they would have burst open with his entrance. He extended his hand as if to shake mine but withdrew his offer as quick as the western fast draw.

"Mr. Hirtle, your wife needs this surgery; I would not do it if I didn't think so. She will be fine." With that he turned and left the room. I stood there stunned. I felt as if I had just been corrected for wetting my pants by my father. I looked around the room and saw that the surgeon's behavior did not have the same impact on the nurses. They had continued business as usual. In a couple of minutes they would take Tammy away. There was nothing I could say to stop it.

After they took Tammy to the operating room I went to the hospital chapel. I cried to God. "Please" was the only word I uttered. After many minutes I left the comfort of the chapel and stood in the hallway outside the operating room's double doors.

A few minutes had passed when I saw nurse number three approaching me. God sends people into our life when we need them the most; nurse number three was sent by God. She asked me if there was something more I needed to tell, she said she didn't believe my apprehension was about the surgery. So I told her everything, starting with the discovery of the empty Vicodin bottles. I told her my suspicions and my concerns, I told her of the many previous visits to the emergency room. She listened without interruption. She then told me she would relay my concerns to the doctor, and that she would pray with me. Her prayer was simple and sincere, she asked God to bring me comfort, bring Tammy strength and to bless my family. I tried to thank her, but couldn't control my trembling lips. She smiled and nodded knowingly. I never saw her after that.

A considerable amount of time passed before I saw the surgeon. He entered the hallway in the same manner he had entered Tammy's room. "Sir, your wife is fine. Her gall bladder was diseased and needed to be removed. The tests do not always reveal everything," he said, justifying his decision. "The nurse told me your concerns. There are people here that can help her get the care she needs." Obviously he did not feel that he was one of these people. With that he shook my hand and left. I would see him only one more time, just for a brief moment. Upon discharging Tammy he came to her room to give her a prescription for

Vicodin. He glanced at me and said, "She will need it, discomfort is common following surgery." He wasn't so John Wayne like upon his exit.

Tammy completed her stay in the hospital and came home with the prescriptions filled. My wife was now officially a drug addict. She had gone to extremes to receive the Vicodin. I suspect that her gall bladder may have eventually become so diseased that surgery was a requirement, but it wasn't this time. I know what you are thinking, *He's not a doctor, how can he know, he doesn't care,* and you are right in that I am not a doctor, but I do care. I care that my wife is capable of convincing doctors that she needs medication for pain all the while concealing her addiction. I care that one day Tammy may go too far, that her desire to go numb will end in her death. I care about the suffering she has gone through, about the anguish she has caused our family, and I care about the pain she has caused me.

"He will wipe every tear from their eyes. There will be no more death or mourning or crying or pain
Revelations 21:4

Suffering Trials

"Consider it pure joy, my brothers, whenever you face trials of many kinds, because you know that the testing of your faith develops perseverance" (James 1:2-3).

Pure joy? If able to sit and speak with the Apostle James, I would ask him to explain this directive. How can we, in the midst of a trial, consider it pure joy? Furthermore, James, why should we consider it as such? His answer is supplied in the following verses, stating that perseverance is developed during the testing of our faith. But I don't want to develop perseverance; I want relief. I want liberation from years of suffering that comes from sharing a household with a drug addict. If the Lord desires to test my faith, then please find another way of application.

David wrote "*Do not bring your servant into judgment, for no one living is righteous before you*" (Psalm 143:2). Father, did you answer his prayer? Will you answer mine? Is this trial a consequence of my behavior? Has my obedience to you fallen short? Is my love for you not enough? Is my faith truly being sure of what I hope for and certain of what I cannot see? (Heb 11:1)

When we go through trials, questions like the ones above have a method of dominating our thoughts. Many times during the last fifteen years, I have asked these questions and many similar to them. The answers to them are not always provided, or when the answer does come, it is not always clear. What is clear to me is where to go to seek the response. Although the Bible does not specifically address every trial we will encounter, it does provide with certainty that the trials will come, *even after the acceptance of salvation.* With study and application, we can find the answers we seek, the comfort we desire and gain assuredness, regardless of the haze caused by the trial.

"I sought the Lord, and he answered me; he delivered me from all my fears" (Psalm 34:4).

Does God answer prayers? I believe He does. I believe the answer is sometimes positioned in His silence. Other times the answer is as evident as the words on this page. The hardest answers for me to understand are the ones that are slow coming, even when the evidence of God's work is apparent. There have been times, when dealing with Tammy's addiction, that I have experienced the intervention of God, without complete closure to a given situation. He provided temporary lodging, shelter from the storm. I knew the winds still blew, the rains continued to fall, but for short periods of time the warmth and comfort of God's grace and mercy prevailed.

But even during these times of comfort, I was still unsure if this trial would end.

"His disciples asked him, 'Rabbi, who sinned, this man or his parents, that he is born blind?' 'Neither this man nor his parents sinned' said Jesus, 'but this happened so that the work of God might be displayed in his life'" (John 9:2-3).

Was the conception of, or the continual suffering a consequence of my actions/sins? Again the Bible is clear concerning the consequence of our sins. The ultimate consequence of our sin, death, was paid for in full by the death and resurrection of our Lord Jesus Christ. In His death and resurrection He allowed us to avoid the eternal separation from God that is the natural result of our sin. God, however, has also allowed us *free will.* When our *free will* places us outside of *God's will*, the consequence may be separation from the grace and mercy of God. The consequence may indeed be unanswered prayer.

"Dear friends, if our hearts do not condemn us, we have confidence before God and receive from Him anything we ask, because we obey His commands and do what pleases Him" (1 John 3:21-22).

If our hearts do not condemn us and because we obey, easier read than done. Our determination to do it our way and not His way allows the suffering and trials we endure to become our focal point. When our focus is not on God, our problems increase, they become insurmountable, they may continue without relief.

"Why do you call me Lord, Lord, and do not do what I say?" (Luke 6:46)

Our loss of focus and disobedience to the Lord is described in a parable of Jesus in the sixth chapter of Luke. Jesus warns us of the storms that will come, but when obedient to Him, we will weather the storm like a well-built house. Without the foundation of faith, the house will collapse under the strength of the storms.

Why was my love for the Lord not enough? I searched for an answer to this question but did not easily find one. Jesus asked Peter three times, *"Do you love me, Peter?"* (John 21) Each time Peter answered yes. With the third reply I can imagine Peter, with tears streaming the weathered face of this fisherman, in frustration proclaiming, "Lord, you know all things! You know I love you!" Christ patiently instructed Peter to do two things, "feed my sheep" and "follow me." He did not say, "Love me more, Peter! Love me and that is enough, Peter." He requires action on our part, that action is evidence of our love for Him. My love for my Lord grows each day, but more important is the evidence of my love. The evidence is what is seen by others. Evidence that should have been shown to Tammy.

Sometimes our prayer, worship and love for our Lord will require further action or obedience on our part. Does this reduce the sovereignty of God? Absolutely not! Like a parent who teaches their child by withholding the desires of the child's heart, God will sometimes teach us in the same manner.

Thankfully, other times God simply says, *"Be still, and know that I am God"* (Psalm 46:10).

Our faith in God is the foundation of our life, our faith that God exists and faith that Christ dying in our place assures our salvation is irrevocable. Our hopes and our relationship with Him ebb and flow. But His steadfastness, His promises, His love, grace and mercy are forever. From the very beginning of time God knew that a day would come when He would tell me to *be still*. He also knew there would be a time when I must listen and change.

I consider now you, dear reader, if it may be a time for change in your life. Whether you have accepted the gift of eternal salvation as offered by the one living God? Have you claimed His promises? If not, there is no better time than this very minute in your life to do so. Put aside my written word and speak to God. Tell Him you know of your sins, and then tell Him that you repent, you turn away from these sins in heart and mind. Tell Him you know that eternal life can only be accomplished through His son Jesus Christ and what He did on the cross over two thousand years ago. He did it for you. Tell Him you accept His gift of Salvation. Thank Him for loving you just as you are. In doing so Jesus Christ is glorified. In doing so, you will know, when you have breathed your last breath, with complete assurance that an eternal life with God in Heaven will begin. Amen.

"He has showed you, O man, what is good. And what does the Lord require of you? To act justly, and to love mercy and to walk humbly with your God."
Micah 6:8

If Change Is Possible

I wrote to you some time earlier that on many occasions I had considered what role I had played in Tammy's addiction. I conveyed to you that I have not found a reason to believe that I am at fault.

As I sit here tonight, I am experiencing an uncertainty in my own beliefs. If I am to believe that I am not the basis, nothing is accomplished in doing so. If I believe that I am the origin, then guilt and self-hatred settles in. But you see the problem lies not in what I believe, but what Tammy believes. Tammy accepts as true that I am the cause. Acknowledging and agreeing with her beliefs may accomplish something; it might, with the grace of God, lead to recovery.

The number of times that Tammy has accused me as being the catalyst of her addiction are too numerous to count or clearly remember. The situations that lead up to her accusations towards me, however, are identifiable. The angry pointing finger is typically displayed during an argument. The initial stages of our arguments are not always about her addiction, or behavior directly associated with the addiction, but they always seem to end up there. Understand, I am very capable of steering the arguments in that direction, especially when I am losing the original debate.

My wanting to blame every situation on her addictive behavior has become so easy. The accelerated argument drives relentlessly to name-calling or the uttering of phrases such as "*I hate you,*" "*Get out of my life*" and other cruel words.

The last decade has included hundreds of these of arguments. I have become unsympathetic to her suggestions that I was fueling her habit. I believed this was her gut reaction used strictly to bring me guilt for having spoken of her addiction. I was certain that her ploy was to misdirect and cause hurt, or deny any responsibility for her dependency on pharmaceuticals.

Being indifferent to her feelings is accompanied by a loss of listening skills. My wife was acknowledging her addiction and I did not hear her. I was more concerned about my words, words designed to cause reciprocal pain, than her cries for help.

James wrote, "*If anyone considers himself religious, and yet does not keep a tight rein on his tongue, he deceives himself and his religion is worthless*" (James 1:26).

The Bible has many teachings on the controlling of our words spoken to others. But in James' statement, it is incredibly clear that we cannot justly claim to follow Christ's ways and continue to use our tongue as a weapon. Tammy has a tremendous memory and frequently quotes me, citing words used in arguments long past. In doing so, it makes it difficult for either of us to stay focused on the matter at hand. My hearing is also muffled by my loss of focus. Tammy believes I am the bad guy, she believes I am the judge and jury and have already convicted her, now just waiting for the sentencing. She believes that I quit caring, quit loving, and quit her. Until today, I did not hear her.

Whether she is correct in her assessment is irrelevant. In her world I am the cause of her problem. How did it ever get to this?

The addict commonly accuses others for their own behavior; in most cases the accusations are false. They justify their addiction by bringing someone else into their dark world. Her world is filled with secrets, secrets that inflict pain on the addict. The pain is forgotten momentarily when the addict is numb, but the ache cannot be destroyed by drugs; it always returns. Desolation desires company, so the addict finds someone to blame, someone to make miserable, hoping that in doing so the unrelenting hurt goes away. When it doesn't they not only ingest more pills but they also increase the volume of accusations, they repeat it over and over. Their lies become their truth.

If I could change something, it would be me. It is easy to say that if granted the opportunity to change the past, I would change Tammy's need to go numb. I can't change the past nor can I change her. God can, but He won't change her without her desire to do so. Changing Tammy can only be accomplished by Tammy. Although not possible retroactively, changing my behavior is part of the equation. Listening, caring and loving, even when it seems impossible to do so, are the changes that must be made. God loves us all the time, even when it is hard to do so. How sad a world it would be if God treated me in the same way I have treated Tammy. What if He chose not to listen to my cries for help as I have ignored hers? Or what if He ignored my problems because He knew that I had brought them upon myself, another stance efficiently accomplished by this author? *Father, teach me to love as you, grant me the patience and understanding that you have shown me. Let my words and my actions guide Tammy back to you, to seek your help, to receive your mercy. Amen.*

I think back to so many occasions when a change in my attitude or actions may have negated Tammy's desire to go numb. Even if a supportive approach had stopped her just once, it would have been one less scar that would need to heal. On the night my family had an impromptu intervention with Tammy, I chose not to participate. After the event was over an argument that ended in mutual silence for days followed. If I had stayed and listened to her cries, instead of assuming her lies, things may have been different. If I had been more loving than demanding the hundreds of times I told Tammy she must stop, perhaps she would have listened. Tammy told me once that dancing in the rain was romantic. Tammy always loved dancing. Our first kiss was while dancing in a small Texas honky-tonk. But dancing in the rain—

romantic? I could just imagine getting wet and cold. But Tammy saw it differently, she saw it as romance. Perhaps if I had listened, maybe if I had taken her in my arms and danced in the rain, looked into her eyes and felt the beat of her heart, then maybe now she would need me more than her desire to go numb.

Finally I would change the way Tammy sees me. When she looks at me she does not see that Christ resides in me. She can't see that I love God and He loves me. She can't see these things because I have not adequately portrayed them. For us to help someone through God, one must see God's remarkable work in our life, constantly and without fade.

God has applied His soothing balm to the thorns in my side many times in my walk with Him. He has been with me when I was at my lowest. He has loved me just they way I am. He never gave up on me, even when I had given up on Him. What God has shown me, a person unworthy of any of his majesty; I must in turn show Tammy. I pray that God will hear this prayer; I pray that I will hear his words.

"Everyone was amazed and gave praise to God. They were filled with awe and said; 'We have seen remarkable things today'" (Luke 5-26).

"I will take refuge in the shadow of your wings until the disaster has passed."
Psalm 57:1

October 30, 2006

I knew this day would eventually come. Friends and family told me this day would come. Experts, former addicts and pastors, all told me this day would come. I have even prayed that this day would come. Fifteen years, to the day, it had finally arrived. Fifteen years ago Tammy woke me to tell me something was wrong. Fifteen years ago the doctors began administering pain pills to my wife, painkillers that since have become Tammy's way of life.

Around the noon hour I received a call from Tammy. She had been arrested. I asked her why, she replied with one word, "prescriptions." This call was not *the one phone call* afforded to those who experience the hallowed halls of our detention systems. That call was still hours away. One of the arresting officers allowed Tammy to make a call from her cell phone prior to confiscating it from her. This highly coveted, yet seldom granted request was allowed after Tammy conveyed the importance of communication with me concerning the safe arrival of our children from school. This call was very brief, four or five words at most were exchanged. The call's brevity is overshadowed by its impact.

I was stunned. I sat in my truck, not moving, not thinking, and maybe not even breathing for what seemed like an eternity.

"Prescriptions" was all she had been able to say. I knew what that meant, I didn't, however, know the details. It would be hours before she confessed that she had forged a prescription for Vicodin, written on a stolen script pad. As she exited the pharmacy with the stolen medication, the police greeted her. This was the beginning of the longest thirty-six hours of our lives.

I mentioned above that I have prayed for this day to come. The prayer was for Tammy to reach *rock bottom* in her life. When I spoke this request it was not driven by desires to cause her harm. It was prayer uttered out of frustration that comes when living with an addict. I hoped, desperately, that if the bottom were reached, Tammy would only be able to look upwards for help.

In team mountain climbing the *leader* has one end of a rope attached to his harness, while the *second* has the other end tied to his harness. The second feeds out the rope as the leader ascends. The second can also cause friction using the appropriate hardware to slow or stop the descent of the leader in the event of a fall, saving his or her life. If the second were to be unsuccessful in his duties, both could fall to their deaths. Hitting rock bottom with Tammy is like the teamed climbers. Tammy is the leader of her life and her choices are her own. I am the second, my duties as a husband and as a father are to cause the friction needed to slow down and stop a descent to the rocky bottom. I chose not to do this. I knew that if the Lord answered my prayer and Tammy hit rock bottom that our children and I would likely fall with her. What was unknown is how each of us would respond. The climb back up would be, without doubt, very difficult for Tammy, but how hard would it be for my children and myself? I have placed my faith in the Lord's mercy and grace. The Bible tells of numerous times of when many were affected by the actions of one, Achan's sin, as example (Joshua, chapters 7-8).

But we also learn that the mercy and grace of God was extended to many through the faith of one, Moses, *"By faith the people passed through the Red Sea, as on dry land"* (Hebrews 11:29). How much more will the grace of God be realized when He knows of the faith of many? A faith system for the family of an addict is critical. My faith team, although not deliberate, has become extensive over the years. As I sat in the truck and the shock began to taper off, I knew I wanted to speak with someone. I knew at this moment, more so than any other time in my life, I needed support, I desired understanding, and I required help. God has provided me with the people who would fill these needs.

My first call was to my eldest sister. The support I required from her involved the caring of my children. I was aware that this day would likely go deep into the night. I suspected that I would be sitting in a room at the city jail, where comfort is not a priority, where people whom societies detest dwell without concern. I would be waiting, perhaps for hours, just waiting. I knew I did not want my children to experience the trepidation that comes when unknowingly waiting. I told Sandy only what I knew and asked her for her help, all the while pondering on who the next call would be placed to.

Tammy's father is a recovering alcoholic, by God's grace sober since 1991, and a paralegal. He knows of Tammy's addiction, to what degree I was unsure. I knew their relationship was strained (the subject of her addiction is avoided at the rare family gathering). I knew that the call to Tammy's father, out of the many calls I would make this day, would be the most difficult. But I also knew that his involvement was needed, his support was desired. I hesitated in calling him, I wouldn't be as confident in my words to him as I had been with my sister. Blessings sometimes are small; this blessing was an answering machine. My message was simple, "Tammy has been arrested, something about prescriptions, please call me."

I did not know who the next call for support should be to. This day, with each call, between each call and after each call I spoke to the Lord. *Give me guidance, Father, give me comfort and be with my wife*, was the prayer repeated over and over. Instead of placing another call I began to drive. My truck was headed in no particular direction; I was not sure where I should go. Tammy had not told me her location; going home seemed like surrender. I tried calling my church, but even churches apparently have answering services. So I drove to the church.

On the drive to the church another person to call occurred to me.

Although this good friend and his wife are not active members of my support team, they have on more than one occasion showed their concern for Tammy, my family and me. They are members of my Bible study group at Trinity Baptist Church. He has involvement in the Alpha Home. I was not sure of his capacity there, or even how he may be able to assist now. Alpha Home was as much as a mystery to me as his involvement. I knew that it was a treatment center that assisted addicts with their problems. I needed to know more, I needed to know if the Alpha Home was an option.

I was able to speak with both my friend and his wife. They provided me with information; more importantly, the provided me with encouragement. Their support did not come only from their kind words; it came also from their listening. I have made my living by speaking to people for many years now. I am very adept at determining when someone is a good listener, when someone is truly listening. These dear friends are true listeners.

I arrived at the church as our conversation was ending. I thanked them for their time and their offers of prayers. Before I exited my vehicle my phone rang. It was Tammy. She had appeared before the magistrate and bail was set at $5,000. She gave me the address of her location. She asked where I was and how long would it be before I would be there. She did this all very matter-of-factly. Where was the remorse or fear I wanted to hear? Where was the pleading for help? Had she survived this ordeal without consequence? Was I wrong for wanting her to feel these things? My concern for her was replaced, no, not replaced, but supplemented with anger. I told her I needed to stop and get the money to post bail, but that I would be there as soon as possible.

I started to drive away, but stopped. I was in the parking lot of the church I attend, the church where I go to celebrate God. My anger at Tammy's cavalier attitude would not stop me from seeking the help I had come here for.

I spoke with John Park, our associate pastor, and also my Bible teacher. I am sure our conversation, one regarding the incarceration of a member's wife for prescription forgery, had never before happened at

Trinity Baptist Church. John Park is a good pastor, but it appeared my circumstances made him uncomfortable. I didn't ask for guidance, or compassion. I simply explained the current circumstances, and for the first time spoke out loud of bailing Tammy out of jail as an option. Saying the words out loud sounded offensive to my ears. Pastor Park did not indicate that it sounded the same to him. The thought of leaving Tammy in her situation had perched itself on the front parapet of my mind from the moment of her first call. We discussed the consequences of the actions I would be taking in the next hour. Compassion and understanding, patience and planning, these were the words offered up by John Park, a man at that moment with a better understanding of God than I. I left the church not knowing what I would do.

As my arrival at the church was interrupted by a phone call, so was my departure. The caller ID reflected only the area code. The call was from a representative from the magistrate's office. Tammy could qualify for a PR bond if I would answer a few questions. I couldn't believe it. He explained to me that Tammy's bail would be reduced to just $150, if I would verify the information she had provided. I did and it was. Her first penalty for the crime committed was reduced to a little more than the cost of a traffic ticket. I had asked God to provide a way to help Tammy make it through this night. He did.

My initial visit to the magistrate's office was brief. Evidently Monday's a slow night for crime fighters. I completed the required paperwork and supplied the money that would be used to free my wife. The desk clerk informed me that it would take six or seven hours to process Tammy out. It would take longer to get her out than the amount of time she had actually been there.

I wouldn't stay, not for six or seven hours. I decided to go home. I thought that some normalcy in my day was deserved. The thirty-minute drive home was occupied with thoughts of what I would say to Tammy when I saw her tonight, of what she would say to me. Would all the truths of the last fifteen years be revealed? Would the remorse missing earlier now surface? Would I be able to control my words? Was this the day that God answered my rock-bottom prayer? I stopped this self-torture long enough to call my sister and check on my children. They were fine and the late-night pickup would be okay.

A police car was parked in front when I arrived. What now, I wondered. The officer and a woman I did not recognize stood by my front door. The woman turned out to be a friend of Tammy's from work; they were concerned when Tammy had not returned from lunch. The officer asked me where my wife was. I looked at him and then at her. "She is in jail," I replied. He asked me her whole name and went to his cruiser. Tammy's friend asked if I remembered her, Tammy and she had been friends since childhood. I apologized and told her I didn't. The officer came back; he had verified the information, and Tammy had been arrested. He said he hoped all would be well then left. Tammy's friend stood there, waiting for me to say more. I remained silent. She told me she knew that Tammy and I were having problems; this is why she called the police. *She thinks I did something to my wife!*

I spoke, "Tammy has a problem, which is why she is in jail." She asked that I have Tammy call her, I told her I would.

My home had never seemed so empty or quiet. I thought I would eat, but I couldn't. I turned on the television; it turned out to be a poor distraction. I opened my Bible. In Psalm 143, David wrote,

"Oh, *LORD, hear my prayer, listen to my cry for mercy; in your faithfulness and righteousness come to my relief.*"

I began to pray.

****

"One of those days Jesus went out into the hills to pray, and spent the night praying to God" (Luke 6:12).

Prayer in our life is uttered for numerous reasons. In thanks, in petition, out of desperation or from ritual. But sometimes, not often, in fact I think rarely, a prayer is said naturally.

The nature of the unsaved man seldom includes prayer. It may embrace wishes or desires for luck, but not prayer. The nature of the saved man, the born-again man, desires to communicate with God. This desire is often tempered by the nature of our old self, the nature of our flesh, which still subsists. But on the rare occasion when all the static and distractions of our old nature subside, a prayer like David's is uttered. I sat in my empty home and read David's cry over and over. As I did, I began to pray David's word to our Lord. My vision was blurred by my tears and at some point I could no longer read the words as written. I said nothing, I became still and I let God be God.

In the fourth chapter of Hebrews, the writer addresses the *rest of God*. Over the years I have studied Hebrews on many occasions. I never gave much thought to the writer's use of the word *rest*. There are differing opinions from the commentators regarding these passages, each sensible and plausible. It is clear that God had been upset with the disobedience of the Israelites. The author was encouraging his audience not to follow their example, "*Let us, therefore, make every effort to enter that rest, so that no one will fail by following their example of disobedience.*" On this night, God's rest became clear to me.

I know now that God's rest can only be experienced with complete surrender. I struggle even now to find the words to describe this rest. Any image I convey to you will be insufficient. Rest in God is like what a small baby must experience when held by his mother, fitting perfectly in a faultless cradle formed effortlessly by her arms, sensing her familiar heartbeat, recognizing her smells and hearing her soothing words. The baby is too young to understand any of his own senses, but it doesn't matter, he is at rest. God's rest is the perfect fit.

For ten minutes that evening I experienced God's rest. For ten minutes I surrendered all to God. For those few minutes I knew what is must be like to be held by our Father, to have no concerns, to know the promises of God, to be at peace with the King of Kings the Lord of Lords, Abba, Father. Then the phone rang.

My moment of peace was interrupted by Carol. She is an administrator at the Alpha Home. She doesn't know my wife or me. I am not sure how she became aware of our situation; perhaps Pastor Park had relayed the information. It didn't matter; I wanted to speak with her. I hoped for answers and solutions. I needed reassurance from one whose vocation includes dealing with drug addicts. After introductions, she asked the first question. Her query surprised me.

She wanted to know how I was doing, what I was going to do tonight.

As I reflect now, I believe my answer to Carol's question was shaped in the minutes prior to her call. God's timing is perfect. Rarely do we understand the perfection of His schedule, and on occasion we may even try to argue with His timetable for our life. At the very moment Carol asked her question, a segment of the peace I felt in the respite of God was revealed to me. I am confident that this revelation would have occurred to me eventually, probably after a time of reflection. But Carol's call became the catalyst to bring to maturity the answer.

How was I? What would I do tonight? I appreciated her concern, but this night was about Tammy. This moment, this situation was about Tammy. For the first time in many years this was not about how her addiction affected our family or me. This would not be another night of bitter arguments filled with words normally uttered in the deepest, vilest places, words that would cut and cause injuries that never completely heal. Today God had begun a work in Tammy's life. Not till the moment of Carol's question did I recognize this. Although I did not understand how, I knew my cries for help were being answered. I knew that if God's attention was on Tammy, then mine must also be.

"This is about Tammy," I answered.

We went on to discuss a number of things. I was impressed, knowing that Carol had never met my wife, that she was able to use the perfect adjectives in describing Tammy. She told me addicts are *manipulative, master liars, cunning and persuasive*. The addict's only concern is the acquisition of their next dose. She told me Tammy likely had a stash somewhere in our home. Carol told me not to expect much tonight in the way of conversation, Tammy had been caught, she will be embarrassed, wanting to withdraw, hide or just disappear. This was the beginning of a new chapter in Tammy's life and how she reacts over the next few hours may determine the outcome.

We spoke of treatment options and the legal implications of Tammy's arrest. This led me to seek Carol's endorsement on my decision to bail Tammy out. Although she was able to avoid a direct response, I easily read between the lines; she did not agree with my decision.

I thanked her for her time and help then hung up. My house was silent, no children laughing or parents fighting, no television blaring its nonsense. Silence, it was peaceful. In a moment I began to enjoy the serene atmosphere. I began to imagine what a life without an addicted wife would be like. I considered the opportunity of starting fresh. What it would be like to make plans again, to have goals, to have some of my own desires filled? My dreams were interrupted again by the ringing of the phone.

It was Tammy. When I heard her voice I was filled with compassion for my wife. My thoughts of just moments ago, still fresh in my mind, were replaced with feelings of guilt. How could I imagine my life without Tammy? She is everything to me; I just want her back, like she was, before those doctors started her on a life of addiction. She told me that she had been released, much sooner than expected, please come pick her up. She was freezing; I told her to go back inside, she said wouldn't. As I drove back downtown I thought of what to say to her. Tammy's life was changing today. This moment in our lives would never be forgotten. What would the results be? Did the arrest frighten her enough to turn away from the drugs? I remembered as a child hearing a radio commercial about drunk drivers. The announcer said to "Scream bloody murder" if you witnessed a drunk driver. Scream for help. Was Tammy screaming? Will she finally realize what the drug was doing to her and her family? So many questions I wanted to ask her.

Our ride home was mostly silent. She spoke little about her time in jail. She complained about the treatment she received, not about getting caught. I asked her if there were any other forgeries; the district attorney probably would find out. She said no. I asked if she had any pills. "No, they took them," she replied.

"I mean do you have any more at home or anywhere else?"

"No," she answered. Nothing else was said.

The next day was Halloween. The thick silence of the previous night continued. I told her that I was taking the children to a party at the church tonight, did she want come? Probably not, she said. I left for work. I told her before leaving that she needed to call her employer. I also told her about the previous night's visit from her friend, that she should call her too. She said she didn't want to speak with anyone. I suggested she call her dad, he is a paralegal, and she may need his help.

"You told my father what happened!"

"I thought he might be able to help."

"That's just fucking great. I can't believe you called him."

I left.

I didn't know that Tammy was beginning to show the signs of chemical withdrawal. It would be a few hours before this became evident to me.

Early that afternoon Tammy called me, she was crying. She told me the pain was too much for her to bear. She was "crawling out of her skin." She couldn't handle this. She needed help. I didn't know what to do. I had spent many hours reading about addictions, yet little effort had been made learning about withdrawals. Julie's warnings from the night before invaded my mind. Was Tammy manipulating me now in order to get drugs? I hadn't thought the withdrawal symptoms would begin this quickly. Tammy's crying was real. I found a doctor close to the house and made an appointment. I told Tammy I would be home soon. "Please hurry," she cried.

All the lights were off, and our house was quiet, unbearably hot. When I saw Tammy I could hardly believe my eyes. She was lying on the bed, curled into a small ball, covered by many blankets. She tried to sit up and barely had the energy to do so. Her skin was the color of cigarette ashes. Her body shook all over. Her eyes were sunken and without color. When I touched her skin it felt dead. Her hair was tangled and sodden with snot and tears. Dear God, what was happening to my wife?

With great effort I was able to get Tammy in the car. She was not responsive to my questions concerning her current condition.

As we drove to the doctor I spoke to Tammy about truth. I stressed to her the importance of complete honesty with the doctor. I told her that if she told the truth, the doctor would not write a script for Vicodin. I told her if he did, we would leave without it. I told her to tell the truth. She did.

The doctor's office was almost empty. The office was new as evidenced by the faint smells of recently purchased furniture, carpets and no out-dated magazines. One mother with her child sat in the uncluttered waiting area. When the mother saw Tammy she held her child closer. Thankfully our stay in the waiting area was brief.

The doctor was young. He paid attention as Tammy spoke, he watched as she twitched and shook. That which was new to the doctor's ears was also new to mine. For the first time I heard Tammy admit to addiction. She told him she took Vicodin and any other painkiller a willing doctor would prescribe. She told him that it started fifteen years ago after major surgery. He listened to every word, not interrupting. When she stopped talking he asked his questions.

"When did you last take any medication?"

"Monday morning."

"How much do you usually take?"

"On a good day, twenty-five to thirty pills, on a bad day forty to fifty."

My heart broke.

"What makes a bad day?"

No answer.

"How do you get that much medication?"

"I see three or four doctors a week."

Doctor shopping.

"Do you have a regular doctor?"

"No. I never see one more than once."

"How do you do that?"

"There are hundreds of doctors and dentists. Finding one is not a problem."

"What is the cause of your pain?"

"There is no pain."

He paused before continuing.

"What brings you here today? Why have you chosen to stop now?"

"I was arrested."

"For what?"

"Forging a prescription."

"How were you able to do that?"

"I worked for a doctor."

"Still?"

"Not anymore."

I was stunned. The doctor didn't appear to be. I didn't know this woman sitting next to me; she sounded like an experienced drug abuser, not the mother of my children. I have greatly underestimated the extent of Tammy's addiction. He asked a few more questions, mostly medical. He went on to tell us that he was not a chemical dependency expert, but that he could recommend one. He told us that he would help Tammy through the withdrawals by prescribing Methadone. I wouldn't find out until later that Methadone's narcotic effect is extremely dangerous, that addiction to this synthetic painkiller is as widespread as Vicodin's. Later I would speak with caregivers at different rehab facilities; their shock to the news that a doctor had prescribed the Methadone was alarming. The doctor told Tammy that I must administer the medication. He told her that she could not be trusted to do it herself. He told her that if she went to another doctor to obtain narcotics, their relationship would end.

As we left the doctor's office Tammy's earlier demeanor had improved. The constant trembling had subsided to almost nothing more than a twitch. She was alert and responsive, even her color improved. All this without drugs; just her knowing the Beast would soon be fed had caused this change.

November 3 (Journal Entry)

The Methadone appears to be working. The symptoms she had shown twenty-four hours earlier have all but disappeared. Her moods are not attractive; the reality of being arrested is taking form. Her attempts to contact the court-appointed attorney have been without success. She has not spoken to anyone, family or friend. I give her the Methadone four times each day; each pill is forty milligrams, which seems like a lot to me. The doctor said it was the equivalent to her Vicodin consumption.

For the first time in almost a year I didn't sleep on the floor, I slept in our bed with my wife.

November 11 (Journal Entry)

Things are not going as I had hoped for. I have tried to talk to Tammy about rehabilitation; she won't listen. She thinks she can do this herself. I have spoken with professionals at different rehab clinics, they tell me she cannot. The continued doses of Methadone help her through most days. Continued prayers help me. She spends most of the day in her room; she has isolated herself from me. We don't talk much. She sends the children to me to get her "nighttime medicine"; they don't understand, they think they are helping Mommy; after all, this is the only time she speaks to them. She did finally speak with the court-appointed attorney. He was not what she expected. I told her he is working for free so don't expect much. Her guilt or innocence is not the question; after all, she was caught red-handed. I told her to hope that he could convince the judge to be as gentle as possible, that's all. He told her he would see her in court. Evidently one phone call is all you get from the free attorney.

November 22 (Journal Entry)

Tomorrow is Thanksgiving. Tammy may not go to our family gathering, she is mad at me. Her Methadone is almost gone; she called the doctor for a refill. He agreed to another thirty-day supply; the pharmacy pointed out to me that thirty days had not passed since the first prescription was filled. The insurance company would not cover the new script, so I had to pay full price. Tammy knows I am upset, but it doesn't matter, she got her drugs. She's mad at me; she thinks I don't care, that I am not supportive of her recovery. What happened to the missing pills?

December 4 (Journal Entry)

We went to court this morning; it was a waste of time. It began with the court-appointed attorney not being on time. When the bailiff announced Tammy's name the attorney was still not present. The court informed us that her attorney had called and said he would be late; thanks for letting us know. He eventually showed up, but by the time he did the judge had adjourned for the morning; they will reset Tammy's court date. The attorney has already discussed Tammy's case with the prosecutor. They would be recommending a three-year adjudicated sentence, a $2,000 fine, two hundred hours of community service and an evaluation by the drug rehab people. Tammy and the lawyer seemed satisfied with the recommendations; I thought they sounded rather forgiving.

December 6

I called 911 today. Tammy's bottle of Methadone was empty this morning. Fifteen days of medication gone, sixty pills, there was no doubting this time. I sat in my truck outside the house for nearly an hour, deciding on what to do. I don't know if she is hiding the pills, or if she was doubling her dose each day. I tried to understand how she had been able to get the pills. I turned this over in my mind. Trying to remember each day since the pharmacy had filled this prescription. I had a routine; I kept the drugs with me all the time. I thought of each day, each night, going over every step. Then I remembered Sunday afternoon. The weather had been nice enough to walk next door to the corner store with my children. They wanted some candy; I agreed to go with them. Tammy was alone for ten minutes, just her and the Methadone. I screwed up, I let my guard down, and she took advantage of the situation. Now the pills were in her possession. A terrible thought began to take form; *what if she took the pills this morning, what if she had swallowed enough to kill herself?* I slowly punched the numbers on my cell phone.

"Nine-one-one, do you need the fire department?"

"No, I think my wife may be trying to kill herself."

I gave her the information she requested, and listened to her directions to me. A police officer and EMS would arrive shortly. I waited outside for their arrival; it didn't take long.

The police arrived first. They asked me standard questions. Before going inside they asked if there were any weapons inside (just drugs, I thought). “No, we don’t have any weapons.”

Tammy didn’t act surprised at the arrival of the police. She would later tell me that these were the same officers that had arrested her for the forged prescription. Tammy acted like the accomplished host of a dinner party; she was polite and friendly, even joking with the officers. One of the officers escorted me out of the bedroom to ask me questions and to allow the other officer to speak with Tammy alone. The first policeman asked me if Tammy had said anything to make me believe she would hurt herself.

“No, but the pills are gone, they were there and now there not.”

“Do you think she would try to hurt herself?”

“That’s why I called. I think she took the pills.” About this time the EMT’s arrived in our home. The police officer directed them to Tammy’s room. He stayed with me and asked more questions; these were less inquiring, address and phone number type of questions. The emergency technicians were with Tammy for about five minutes. They had taken her vitals and were asking her questions of their own. After they finished one of them came to me and repeated the questions the policeman had asked just moments ago. “I think she took the Methadone. It was there and now it’s gone. She is a drug addict. I think she took the pills.” I went back into Tammy’s room with one of the techs; she asked Tammy if she took the pills.

“No.”

“Then where are the pills?”

“I took them.”

“You just said you didn’t.”

“I didn’t take them today. I have been taking more than prescribed amount each day. But I didn’t take them today.”

“Why did you take more than you were supposed to?”

“Nerves.”

With that, everything was suddenly over. The tech told me her vitals were good, she told me we should probably seek drug counseling for Tammy. Helpful advice. The policeman then informed me that thinking about killing oneself was not illegal, that unless an attempt was made there was nothing they could do.

"So if she kills herself, I should call you then."

"That's correct." More helpful advice.

"Even though I walk through the valley of the shadow of death, I will fear no evil, for you are with me."
Psalm 23:4

December 26, 2006

Tammy is in the care of Laura Ridge Hospital. She is under suicide watch. A lot of things have led up to today, events that I have not yet written about. I will go back and fill in the blanks, but I need to record this now, while everything is fresh in my mind. I need to convey to you as clearly as possible the events of the last three days. I do not know if you are an addict, or if like me, you are the victim of an addict, nevertheless, the following words are written for the addict. I want you, the addict, to understand what your choices do to your family. I want you to feel the pain that derives from your behavior. I want the knots in my stomach and the fear in my mind to be yours. Merry Christmas.

Christmas is the time of year that should be filled with wonderful music, with anxious children anticipating a morning that would reveal presents under the brightly lit Christmas tree. It should be a time of worshiping and celebrating the birth of our Savior, visiting family and friends, sharing deliciously fattening foods, drinking eggnog and wrapping gifts; these things should have their beginnings as memories today. Instead my memories of Christmas 2006 will be the ones I will forever struggle to forget.

On the eve of Christmas Eve Tammy was at her worst. The night before, I had taken her to her second meeting with Narcotics Anonymous. She wanted me to attend with her but I didn't. Her participation at this particular meeting was planned at the last minute and I had already made arraignments to go to our family Bible study. After her meeting, her frustration with me continued when I told her we could not go to a late movie. It was three days before Christmas; I had no extra money and still needed to buy gifts for our children. We went to bed, not talking, each of us as close to the edge of our respective sides as possible.

The next morning I did attend the NA meeting with her; it was December 23, just hours away from Christmas Eve. After the meeting I asked her if she wanted to go shopping with me; she said no, she was feeling light-headed and nauseous. I should have recognized these early warning signs.

Later that evening, Tammy begged me to take her to the emergency room; she couldn't get in touch with her pain management doctor. She called another pill dispenser, her newest general care doctor; she recommended Tammy go to the ER. Tammy was having an anxiety attack unlike any previous. The cause of her anxiety was unstated; although I suspect that either her anger at me or the need to medicate was the origin. The latter more likely, but I could not dismiss the former.

My memories of this Christmas will be filled with (in no particular order) sitting in a room with fifteen or so recovering addicts lamenting over their villainous past; driving to the hospital in cold and rainy weather wondering how long this visit would last; watching Tammy shake while lying in the fetal position as a nurse attempted to start an IV; wondering what I would tell my children about this trip to the hospital; watching as a second, more skilled nurse poked at her veins, struggling to insert the needle that would carry the relief Tammy so desired; wondering what my children would remember about this Christmas Eve; listening to another doctor explain why he would not dispense a narcotic yet Tammy leaving with prescriptions designed to bring weekend relief. My memories will include a Christmas Day visit to my family without Tammy, having to explain over and over why my children's mother was not enjoying this special occasion with them. Memories of Tammy directing my eleven-year-old daughter to sneak her pills out of my coat pocket while I was using the bathroom; her taking those same prized pills before the prescribed time; memories of her slurred speech when my older daughter and grandchildren came to visit on the evening of Christmas Day, their stay being cut short when the tension in the room caused by Tammy's condition became too great to bear. Memories of the police knocking on my door this morning looking for Tammy, explaining to me that she had again called her pain management doctor, crying, asking the doctor to call in a script for Vicodin. Memories of the police telling me that when the doctor refused her request Tammy threatened to kill herself. Informing me that Tammy had given a false address to the doctor (the reason for this particular deception still remains a mystery), and they wanted to know where Tammy was now. Remembering always what a protective order is and what it means to my family. Memories of my children standing in the living room, still littered with the few Christmas gifts they received, crying and afraid that the police would take Mommy to jail. Added memories will span the following five hours of knowing nothing of the condition of my wife; memories of the therapist telling me that she was unable to relay anything to me without the consent of my wife—the addict. Memories of Tammy calling me three times in five minutes, first accusing me of having her locked up, second to tell me "fuck off" and third simply to say "good bye."

All of this, because of a pill. I hope by reading my memories it will prevent you from inflicting the same pain on someone you love. I hope that my writing skills are sufficient enough that you feel this pain. Merry Christmas.

****

December 28, 2006

I went back to read what I had written on the night of December 26. I did so not to refresh my faltering memory, the events of these three days are very clear, but I did so to insure that I won't forget the pain I felt. This pain resulted in a loss of focus. I told you earlier that on occasion I have left God outside, not seeking His comfort or His guidance. The words recorded on December 26 are evidence of this dangerous self-centered behavior. With His grace I have reestablished my focus. I told you that all events leading up to Christmas Day had not been recorded and promised to do so. I would be unable to fulfill my promise if not for the Word of God. The Apostle Paul wrote, "*Let all bitterness, and wrath, and anger, and clamour, and evil speaking be put away from you...*" (Eph. 4:31). Proverb 14:10 gently teaches us, "*Each heart knows its own bitterness, and no one else can share its joy.*" When we are bitter, consumed by the pungent nature of our situation, we cannot recognize, much less share, the joys that are in our life. God is the joy in my life, so I put away my bitterness and anger and tell you rest of the story.

December 9, 2006

Tammy had been without the Methadone for two days before the withdrawals began. I had read that the drug stayed in the body for three days, but her appearance indicated otherwise. Another trip to an emergency room was made. There were more explanations about her addiction, heard by more caring doctors. The doctor told Tammy she was through the most difficult part of the withdrawals, that it would get easier from here, then more prescriptions written. The Methadone had replaced the Vicodin, and now anti-anxiety drugs and anti-depressants replaced the Methadone. Enough would be provided for her to make it through the weekend. These new drugs had unfamiliar names. Would they be addictive? The prescriptions were written with the understanding that Tammy would seek help through a treatment center and the recommendation that she follow up with her doctor.

December 11, 2006

Tammy kept her promise to the doctor and we went to Laurel Ridge Treatment Center this morning. We were interviewed by the staff nurse. She asked few but probing questions and Tammy answered them all without shame, hesitation or deceit. Today is a good day. I hope this will be the starting point of her climb up from rock bottom. Obstacles did appear today when dealing with the insurance company. The treatment center offers an inpatient program and two outpatient programs. The insurance company chose to authorize the least significant, a three-hour outpatient program. Their decision was made after a five-minute conversation with the staff nurse; following her ten-minute conversation with Tammy. Fifteen years of addiction and Tammy's treatment plan is determined in mere minutes by strangers. Strangers who know nothing of the pain Tammy has caused herself and her family. I am not satisfied, but I am grateful. God is beginning a work in Tammy's life. I don't have to understand or even be satisfied. Today is a good day.

December 13, 2006

Tammy started treatment today at Laurel Ridge. When I asked her how it went her reply was less than encouraging. She thought the other patients there would be like her, but they weren't. We like to assemble with people who are the same as us. Their drugs of choice ranged from alcohol to crack, although some were similar to Tammy's. Their reasons for being there were as diverse. Some voluntary, some court ordered, and others as a last result before their families disown them. I think a few of the patients scared Tammy. She did not disclose what was talked about or the designs of the program. I hope things will get better.

December 14, 2006

After leaving the treatment center today Tammy had an appointment with a pain management doctor. I am not sure why this appointment was made; perhaps it is a part of her recovery. I do know this however; I do not like the results of this appointment. Tammy left with four new prescriptions; Ambien for insomnia, Ativan for anxiety disorder, Effexor for depression and Klonopin for panic disorders. This cocktail of new drugs concerns me. The internet is such a great tool; you can discover information on about any subject imaginable. The information about these drugs I obtained from an online PDR is disheartening. The information included terms such as tolerance and dependence, drugged feeling, nausea, coordination problems, depression and reduced thinking ability. The side effects aptly describe my wife before taking the drugs. I fear these drugs will increase the problems associated with fifteen years of painkiller abuse and decrease the reasoning ability she will need to fully recover. I called the pen wielding prescription writing doctor, they won't talk to me, patient privacy.

"Our Father in Heaven, hallowed is your name."
Matthew 6:9

December 23, 2006— The Higher Power

I accompanied Tammy to the NA meeting this morning. This is Tammy's third meeting; it was my first. I wasn't sure what to expect; she had shared very little with me from the first two meetings. That which she did share was not encouraging.

Sixteen addicts and I occupied the room. The aroma of fresh coffee and Christmas tamales filled the air. Little conversation was heard in the room. It is two days before Christmas and no talk of the usual holiday cheer was perceptible. The chairman asked if there were any first-timers; no one raised their hand. He then queried if there were any visitors; I did not raise my hand.

As I looked around the room I couldn't help to be curious about the stories of the addicts gathered here today. If you were to encounter any of them on the street or in the workplace, in the mall or at a church, you would not know they were drug addicts. But assembled collectively there was a discernable tell on each of their faces. Their eyes. In those eyes I could see the pain of the possessors past. I sensed their reluctance to meet the gaze of any fellow addicts, even more so the new stranger in their midst. As if by avoiding eye contact they could shield their truth from the world. But the lone truth that matters was revealed in their attendance at a Narcotics Anonymous meeting; they are addicts.

The chairman began by having others read from a litany of stamped and well-practiced statements. The statements told of the addict's surrender, some told of the responsibility of the addicted in his or her recovery. They spoke of a god, a higher power, or a god of their understanding. They did not speak of God, Jesus Christ or the Holy Spirit. Perhaps in order to be reasonable and equal, they require their god to remain anonymous too. They read aloud about anonymity. With anonymity, their stories, the pain they caused themselves, the hurt they inflicted upon their loved ones, their gods, and their goals, would all remain in the confines of this room where rent is paid weekly by the meager contributions of an addict. Disregard of anonymity pledges would result in poor consequences for the betrayer. I wondered if the consequence of anonymity also contributes to the frequent addiction relapse.

The floor was then opened for the addicts to share their stories. Guidelines are established for the telling of these stories. The element of their tales that would have gained my curiosity was not revealed. How did it begin, which drug, how much, how many relapses, whose life had they damaged; all questions left unanswered.

One addict rambled on about the need to attend these meetings every day of the week. Without a meeting, he would use again. Another confessed that at these meetings he always told the same tale, it was the only one he had, and anything else would be a lie. His story was decorative; every third or fourth word one normally reserved for restroom-wall graffiti. I am not a prude, nor do I concern myself if someone selects filth as his second language; this is his business. But because of this addict's abuse of the English language, I was unable to fully comprehend what he actually spoke about.

A few more addicts mumbled through brief monologues, barely heard by anyone.

The chairman then moved onto the next order of business. Was anyone facing a current situation that may cause him or her to use again? The same addict who had earlier confessed his need for daily meetings raised his hand. A fat man sitting to his right, silent to this point, instructed the owner of the raised hand that the rules allowed a member to share only once during a meeting. Amazingly as the moment had arrived when an addict was reaching out for help he was swiftly spanked on the virtual wrist and told to be quiet. These people have been breaking rules their whole life; what would one more infraction mean? *Let him talk!* The very design of these meetings is to help; yet when one of their own attempted to cry out he was hushed. I glanced around the room to look for outrage or sympathy, empathy, anything! But I saw none and the meeting proceeded. More items were read aloud by pre-selected volunteers, with the remaining members chanting the familiar phrases in choir-like fashion. A reminder to proceed "One day at a time" was announced, followed by a group hug and attempt at prayer. The meeting was over.

Our walk back to the car was in a cold and dreary rain, only silence passed between Tammy and me. As the car warmed so did the mood. I asked Tammy what she thought of this meeting. "The same as the others," she replied.

"Will you go again?" I asked.

"I have to; four times a week is required by Laurel Ridge."

The remaining trip home included little conversation, none of it regarding the meeting. The silence on the trip home and subsequent continued silence at home afforded me the opportunity to process this recent experience. By Tammy's accord, all three meetings thus far attended were similar. The reading of the narcotic's stanzas was customary at each. Solicitation of stories, group hugs, recognizing days of sobriety by the handing out of key fobs, each affair repeated at every meeting. As I replayed the meeting over and over I struggled to recognize the benefits of attending. Perhaps the redundancy was for the benefit of first-timers. (There were none today, except me.) Yet if this is the case, how would they ever proceed beyond the first step?

I began to consider one of the last things read, something about "One day at a time." The strength and understanding of this simple statement became clear all at once. Fighting the entangling power of the addiction is a battle that must be fought by the abuser one day at a time. More importantly, to the addict each day must be considered a new day, a fresh beginning. Each new day a disjointing from the past life of drug abuse and the new life of sobriety widens. For the addict to be successful she must have routine. A routine that replaces the habit; ironically the superfluous nature of the NA meeting provides that routine.

Throughout the afternoon I would replay the meeting over in my head. Dissecting it piece by piece would be required to gain further understanding of my wife's new attendant. The use of the terms "higher power" and "god as I understand him" continued to plague my thoughts. If the addict knows the one true God of the universe, if she has accepted Jesus the Christ as her savior and redeemer, if she has experienced the grace and mercy of God; then why call Him by any other name? Higher power? Luke Skywalker recognized a Higher Power—the Darkside. Faith is all that is required in knowing God, not *understanding Him*. There are mysteries in the Bible that we may never understand. Just as there are events in our lives that will always remain ambiguous. Understanding God will come as our relationship with Him grows. As we learn to trust Him more the omnipotence of God will be revealed. The addict must stop minimizing God, stop putting Him in a brown plastic pill bottle, where darkness conceals the contents, stop opening the bottle to peer inside only when it is convenient for you. For God's sake, stand in your chair and claim that you know the one and only Jesus Christ. Get on your knees and thank Him for pulling you out of the darkest time of your life, ask Him for mercy, ask Him to help you continue *one day at a time*.

Each of us, including the addicted, has two incredible gifts available for our taking. One gift is a powerful mind. The addict's mind has been altered by years of abuse, but the power that was there before the addiction still remains. It may be bruised or buried deep, but it is still there! You were once able to say "No." Except for the innocent babies born to addicted mothers the need to go numb or get high hasn't always been there. The addict must find that power; you control your thoughts, your actions and your reactions. "Just say no" may sound cliché, but it works, even when you are speaking to yourself. The powerful mind is a gift from God. God honors our free will as much as He loves us. He honored your free will when you chose a life of addiction; He will honor your free will when you choose to stop. He will be there through the withdrawals, through the temptations, and through the failures.

The second gift *is God*. All you have to do is turn around and accept His gift. God sent his only Son to die for you. In His dying you were saved. If you were the only one in all of time to accept this gift of everlasting life, Jesus would still have carried the cross, and he would have still felt the guard's whip opening the flesh on his back. He would have still suffered the pain of spikes driven through His hands and feet. He still would have endured the searing pain of a spear in His side, and Jesus Christ still would have looked into the Heavens and asked His Father to forgive you. He still would have cried, "It is finished. " He would have done all this for you. He loves you.

NA meetings, antidepressant drugs, sleeping pills, and support groups may all be needed in the recovery stages of an addict. But going from one dependency to another can be avoided. These gifts have your name written on them; please, Tammy, just take them.

December 29, 2006

Well, dear reader, you are now up to date. Tammy will be released from Laurel Ridge today. The doctor has added another drug to her daily cocktail. This newest ingredient is the drug Zyprexa. Zyprexa manages the manic phase of bipolar disorder. I did not know my wife was bipolar. Do the doctors know?

Yesterday I emailed my insurance company. I told them that my wife was now in full care of Laurel Ridge. I told them that if they had approved more than a token care program three weeks ago perhaps she would not have threatened suicide. I told them that the professional consensus seems to be that drug addicts suffer from a disease. A disease that is able to convince the addict that they do not have a disease. I told them that it appears that it is only convenient for them to refer to the addiction as a disease when the fiscal responsibility lies with someone else. I questioned if any other disease, cancer by example, would be approved for only token medical care. I was surprised that they responded. After many hours on the phone, approval was granted to allow Tammy to attend the full-day outpatient program beginning next week.

God continues His work, one day at a time.

"Against all hope, Abraham in hope believed."
Romans 4:18

Day 30

Tammy believes this is her thirtieth day of sobriety; a milestone in the life of a drug addict, a milestone that she is proud of. *Sobriety* as defined in her case is being free from Vicodin and Methadone. Sobriety evidently doesn't mean drug free. It would be useless and probably detrimental for me to point out the fact that she has really only changed drugs, so I don't.

Other things have also changed over the last thirty days, some good, some not so good. I am committed to be compassionate and support her efforts, but I cannot ignore the five prescribed medications that she ingests each day. I will never be able to forget the day that her doctor handed her the refill prescription just moments after accusing her of abusing the very drugs he was prescribing. The same doctor looking her in the eye and calling her a liar, after she had told me that she was allowed to monitor her own drug intake as part of the treatment program. Is he a doctor or a pusher? The addictive nature of the new pills may be different than the Beast of old, but at the end of the day, they are still drugs, swallowed by a drug addict. I cannot ignore that she sometimes stays awake all night, clutching herself, complaining of being cold even when the heat in our home is unbearable for the rest. Her lack of sleep is unexplainable when I consider that the amount of pills swallowed should render anyone comatose. I can't ignore when she slurs her words after the drugs have begun their work, or when she can't remember the day of the week, or to turn off the stove. She is sometimes confused about where or when; she asked me yesterday if I had heard from Elizabeth, our daughter, she wanted to know if she had gone into labor…our grandson is a year old. I do not think that the combination of these medications is the solitary source of her confused behavior. I am afraid that she is abusing these new meds, causing an unsullied numbness. My children look at their mother with their eyes sometimes filled with compassion, at other times with shame.

God please forgive me, I liked my wife better when she just abused Vicodin.

Each night I pray for Tammy; when done I wipe my tears and then pray again. I just want God to be done with this.

Tammy still attends Laurel Ridge Hospital, now as an outpatient. The bills are piling up. I can't ignore the countless NA meetings and doctor appointments that Tammy must attend to continue her road to recovery, just as I can't ignore her addictive yearning to attend these same meetings.

In 1973-74, the Mighty Golden Bears were playing against the Chargers of Churchill. At halftime the score was 55-0; we of the Golden Bear clan were behind. Not a single person on the field, in the locker room or in the stands believed that the Bears could win this game. Yet when the third quarter began the players entered the field to accomplish what they had come there to do. The teams went through the motions of playing a football game all the while knowing what the final outcome would be. Late in the third quarter the Golden Bears did score, the cheers were obligatory with little enthusiasm. But on the sideline I spied one excited person, the head coach. In his excitement I detected a glimmer of hope. The coach knew that on this night a win for his team would not happen, yet for one brief moment he held onto hope.

My life has been like that game played so many years ago. Most days I fear I know what my wife's outcome will be, yet I keep running back on the field. I feel as though I am only going through the motions of life. My concerns for Tammy have power over me. Everything else, my family and my job become background noise. But every so often, like the score that provided Coach with that brief moment of hope, something happens that grants me the same small hope. Sometimes Tammy has a good morning or shows progress in her effort towards sobriety. When she isn't good, I open my Bible and seek the comfort and reassurances of God's word. Occasionally it requires hours of reading and meditation before the hope is revealed to me, but each time the hope has come.

Tammy believes this is her thirtieth day clean; it is the thirtieth day of my new role—the husband of a recovering addict. I will learn new ways to be supportive and be the understanding companion. I will include in my morning prayer, petitions for Tammy to realize the benefit of sobriety. I will pray that with each new day, a piece of Tammy from years past will recover (as I reluctantly accept that this may never happen). I will learn to recognize that being the prime support for the recovering addict is a full-time position, that the fine line between recovery and relapse is easily crossed when my support for her weakens. If I could shield her from every negative influence I would; I love her. But I cannot always be her shield bearer; the world around us continues, not caring about the addicted.

Tammy believes this is her thirtieth day clean, and for you, my friend, it marks the end of this tale. The conclusion will not be defined as happy or sad. Minus the manuscript my story will continue one day at a time.

When looking to publish I was asked to detail what my book was about. I said it began as a story about living with an addict, and retelling of the pains endured. The story would include seeking answers through scripture. The book is about addictions, doctors, rehab and God. But the simplest answer was to say it is about faith. Faith in knowing that without God Tammy would be dead; faith in knowing that even when I felt as if I could not go on, with God's grace I did; faith that unanswered prayers are not unheard prayers. In this writing experience I have come to understand more clearly about faith. My faith and my relationship with Jesus Christ have matured. I still don't know the why, but I know God.

If reassurance is what you sought in reading these words, I have not been able to offer much. The grim statistics that follow the recovering addict have not changed. Every day someone relapses. Every day someone begins his or her quest to go numb. Every day someone dies from swallowing too many pills or smoking too much crack, or slitting her wrists. But perhaps, with faith, those statistics will change. I hope that as my faith gained form in the writing of these words, so yours formed in the reading.

As you lay this book down for the last time, and Tammy comes to mind, I ask for your prayers, each day is a challenge for her and my family. I pray sharing my journey it has helped you in some way. Perhaps you won't repeat my mistakes. Perhaps you will draw closer to God.

As I leave you, I pray, that you or your loved one will never experience the life that comes with *going numb*.

"And the peace of God, which transcends all understanding, will guard your hearts and your minds in Christ Jesus."
Philippians 4:7
Amen

Epilogue

February 5, 2007

Last night Tammy overdosed on her medications. I walked into our bedroom and found her lying on the floor. Next to her was an empty pill bottle. I called for an ambulance. Just as that night so many years ago, the closed doors of the ambulance separated me from my wife. She is the hospital now. She is unaware of her surroundings. She didn't know who I was. The doctors are doing their best, the have assured me that her condition is not life threatening. They can't answer my questions about her mind. They will run more tests, take more blood, and administer more medications. The circle is now complete; Tammy is numb.

I will continue to pray and seek His help. My prayers have changed during this journey, I have learned more about addictions, about recovery and who they affect. I have learned whom to pray for. So now my prayers include a request that Tammy will again one day celebrate Day One.

October 2007

Sometime ago I warned you that if left to its own this story may never end. It has taken longer to put this book in your hands than I thought. God's timing has once again shown to be superior to my own. For now I have the opportunity to share with you two events that have occurred during this pause.

My sister, Susie, died in August. Her body finally succumbed to the years of alcohol and drug abuse. Her soul is home with her Savior. The last weeks of her life were spent in a hospital bed. The We Care People weren't much different here than in the other hospitals, vague in their answers, professional in their care, all the while with looks of disdain on their faces as they cared for another addict. For one week Susie appeared to be on the way to recovery. She sat up in bed, ate small amounts of food, snapped at the nurses and even occasionally spoke of the future. Most importantly, these few days that God granted to Susie and our family, a brief time of fellowship, allowed her son to share the news that he and his wife would soon be having their first child. Sue smiled.

The second event is Tammy's recovery. Tammy has been drug free for more than six months now. She works full time with me. She occasionally comes to church, and now regularly attends family bible study. God has begun a work in her life that I am too small to see. I am comforted by simply knowing that He is working in our lives. He will defeat evil, even when evil is that seemingly unbeatable foe-addiction. Thank you God, You made Tammy smile.

Jim Hirtle